本冊 Lesson 1 の英文をもう一度読んで，次の活動に取り組みましょう。

Words and Phrases

英文中に出てきた語句・表現について，それぞれ左側の空所には英語を，右側の空所には日本語に意味を書き入れましょう。

1. be about to 〜　_____
2. leave for ...　_____
3. study abroad　_____
4. _____　名 [A2] フライト
5. _____　副 [A2] どこかで

6. _____　副 [A2] 実際は
7. look around ...　_____
8. _____　副 [A1] 注意深く
9. _____　副 [A2] その代わりに
10. definitely 副 [B1]　_____

Questions

次の問いに英語で答えましょう。

1. Where is Routa now?

_____

2. What does Routa need for his flight?

_____

3. Where are Routa's passport and boarding pass?

_____

4. What did Routa leave at home?

_____

Express Yourself

あなたが朗太になったつもりで，タブレット PC を受け取ったお礼とニューヨークでの生活を報告するメールを，書き出しに続けて30語程度の英語で書いてみましょう。

From	Routa
To	_____
Subject	Thank you for sending me my tablet PC
Hi!　I'm so happy _____	
_____	
_____	
Kind regards,	
Routa	

HINTS　①タブレットパソコンを受け取ったこと，②ニューヨークの生活は楽しい，③友達ができた，などの要素を入れるとよいでしょう。

Helpful Expressions　be happy to 〜「〜してうれしい」　　enjoy one's life「生活を楽しむ」
make friends with ...「…と友達になる」

本冊 Lesson 2 の英文をもう一度読んで，次の活動に取り組みましょう。

Words and Phrases 英文中に出てきた語句・表現について，それぞれ左側の空所には英語を，右側の空所には日本語の意味を書き入れましょう。

1. amazing 形 [B1] ....
2. be famous for ... .
3. unique 形 [B1] ....
4. .... 形 [A2] 国立の
5. .... 形 [A2] ふつうでない

6. .... 形 [A1] …ごとに
7. from A to B ....
8. .... 名 [A1] 券
9. look for ... .
10. accommodation 名 [B2] ....

Questions 次の問いに英語で答えましょう。

1. According to the notice, what can we watch in Australia?

....

2. What animals does Daintree National Park have?

....

3. Where can we buy a tour bus ticket?

....

4. How much will it cost if we buy tickets for two adults and one ten-year-old child?

....

Express Yourself あなたはある動物園で一日券 (one-day ticket) を購入します。動物園スタッフとの会話の流れに合うように，下線部に英語を書きなさい。

You: Excuse me, but ① .... one-day tickets?

Staff member: You can buy them here.

You: ② ....

Staff member: $15 for an adult and $8 for a child over 3. You don't need a ticket for a child under 3.

You: Thank you. Then, ③ ...., please?

Staff member: OK. That'll be $46 for the four tickets.

You: Thanks!

HINTS スタッフの返答の内容をヒントにして会話の流れをつかみましょう。

Helpful Expressions Can I buy [get] ...?「…を買うことができますか。」 How much is it [are they]?「いくらですか。」

本冊 Lesson 3 の英文をもう一度読んで，次の活動に取り組みましょう。

Words and Phrases 英文中に出てきた語句・表現について，それぞれ左側の空所には英語を，右側の空所には日本語の意味を書き入れましょう。

1. It seems that ... _____
2. total 形 [B1] _____
3. at most _____
4. researcher 图 [B1] _____
5. at least _____

6. _____ 副 [A2] それゆえに
7. in 〜ing _____
8. as ... as possible _____
9. spend ... 〜ing _____
10. get better at ... _____

Questions 次の問いに英語で答えましょう。

1. According to the passage, do all junior high school and high school students in Japan have to study English at school?

_____

2. According to some researchers, how many hours do learners need to learn English?

_____

3. What is important in learning English?

_____

4. If we spend more time using English, what will happen?

_____

Express Yourself 次の質問について，あなたの考えとその理由を30語程度の英語で書いてみましょう。

Question: What is a good way to learn English?

_____

_____

_____

[HINTS] 効果的な英語学習の方法を自分で考えてみましょう。例えば，「英語圏の国の文化に詳しくなる」や「英語で映画を観る」などが考えられます。A good way to learn English is to 〜 の形で英文を始めるとよいでしょう。

[Helpful Expressions] become familiar with ... 「…に詳しくなる」
make friends with international students 「留学生と友達になる」
read English news on the Internet 「インターネットで英語のニュースを読む」

本冊 Lesson 4 の英文をもう一度読んで，次の活動に取り組みましょう。

Words and Phrases　英文中に出てきた語句・表現について，それぞれ左側の空所には英語を，右側の空所には日本語の意味を書き入れましょう。

1. _____ 動 [A2] …を注文する
2. Thank you for ~ing _____
3. _____ 副 [A2] 不運にも
4. _____ 副 [A2] オンラインで
5. _____ 副 [A2] その代わりに

6. taste 图 [B1] _____
7. fragrance 图 [B2] _____
8. cancel 動 [B1] _____
9. make sure that ... _____
10. specify 動 [B2] _____

Questions　次の問いに英語で答えましょう。

1. According to the e-mail, why can Marie not get the orange tea?

_____

2. What can the company send to Marie instead of the orange tea?

_____

3. Why does the company believe Marie would like the lemon tea?

_____

4. If Marie wants to order the lemon tea, what should she tell the company?

_____

Express Yourself　マリエになったつもりで，Lesson 4 の E メールの中でたずねられていることに答える返信メールを，30語程度の英語で書いてみましょう。

Subject:	Re: About your order
From:	Marie Saito
To:	David Moore (British Tea in London)

Dear David Moore,

_____

_____

Best,

Marie Saito

HINTS　まずはメールをしてくれたことに対する感謝を述べましょう。そして，レモンティーを頼むのか，注文をキャンセルするのかを書きましょう。レモンティーを頼む場合は，メールでたずねられた情報を伝え，キャンセルする場合はその理由などを書くとよいでしょう。

Helpful Expressions　Thank you for e-mailing me. 「メールをしてくれてありがとう。」
Could you send me ...? 「…を送っていただけますか。」
order 100 grams of the lemon tea 「レモンティーを100グラム注文する」
need it by ... 「それを…までに必要です」

本冊 Lesson 5 の英文をもう一度読んで，次の活動に取り組みましょう。

Words and Phrases

英文中に出てきた語句・表現について，それぞれ左側の空所には英語を，右側の空所には日本語の意味を書き入れましょう。

1. _____ 名 [A1] 映画館
2. _____ 形 [A1] それぞれの
3. in advance _____
4. icon 名 [B2] _____
5. available 形 [B1] _____

6. proceed to ... _____
7. purchase 名 [B2] _____
8. _____ 前 [A2] …を持たないで
9. wait in line _____
10. _____ 形 [A1] 奇妙な

Questions

次の問いに英語で答えましょう。

1. If the face icon is shown on the calendar, what does it mean?

_____

2. According to the table on the website, what is the title of the fantasy movie?

_____

3. Which movie is the longest of the three?

_____

4. Who can see the night shows?

_____

Express Yourself

次の質問について，あなたの考えとその理由を30語程度の英語で書いてみましょう。

Question: What is your favorite movie?

_____

_____

_____

HINTS 自分のお気に入りの映画について，My favorite movie is ... から文章を始めて表現してみましょう。

Helpful Expressions
a hit movie「(映画の) ヒット作」 plot「あらすじ」
from a cultural point of view「文化的な観点から」 fully enjoy ...「…を存分に楽しむ」
the lines are impressive「セリフが印象的である」
the movie scenes are beautiful「映画の映像がきれいである」

本冊 Lesson 6 の英文をもう一度読んで，次の活動に取り組みましょう。

Words and Phrases 英文中に出てきた語句・表現について，それぞれ左側の空所には英語を，右側の空所には日本語の意味を書き入れましょう。

1. _____ 图 [A2] 飛行
2. look forward to ... _____
3. _____ 图 [A1] 休暇
4. _____ 形 [A2] その土地の
5. pick ... up _____

6. _____ 图 [A1] 空港
7. No problem. _____
8. _____ 動 [A2] くつろぐ
9. wake ... up _____
10. _____ 图 [A1] 違い

Questions 次の問いに英語で答えましょう。

1. What does Robert want Frank to do?

_____

2. How long does it take from Frank's house to the airport by car?

_____

3. What will Robert do while he is waiting for Frank?

_____

4. What country does Robert probably live in?

_____

Express Yourself 次の質問について，あなたの考えとその理由を30語程度の英語で書いてみましょう。

Question: Which do you prefer, traveling by train or traveling by plane?

_____

_____

_____

HINTS 電車は「移動時間はかかるが本数が多い」，飛行機は「移動時間は短いが搭乗に時間がかかる」など，それぞれのメリット・デメリットを考えてみましょう。

Helpful Expressions check in at the airport「空港で搭乗手続きをする」　destination「目的地」
enjoy the view from the train [the plane]「電車[飛行機]からの景色を楽しむ」
get on board「搭乗する」　prefer ～ing「～するほうが好きだ」　save time「時間を節約する」

本冊Lesson 7の英文をもう一度読んで，次の活動に取り組みましょう。

Words and Phrases 英文中に出てきた語句・表現について，それぞれ左側の空所には英語を，右側の空所には日本語の意味を書き入れましょう。

1. _____ 图 [A2] 掲示　　　　　6. _____ 動 [A2] …を運営[管理]する

2. annual 形 [B1] _____　　　　7. farewell 图 [B1] _____

3. participant 图 [B1] _____　　8. _____ 形 [A2] 基本的な

4. in order to ～ _____　　　　9. _____ 動 [A2] 申し込む

5. in addition to ... _____　　　10. fill out ... _____

Questions 次の問いに英語で答えましょう。

1. According to the notice, where will the Group Discussion Program be held?

_____

2. How many people from Japan will join in the Group Discussion Program?

_____

3. When will the participants give their presentations on global warming?

_____

4. According to the notice, what will be held at the Conference Center?

_____

Express Yourself ボランティアに応募するにあたり，次の申込書を記入する必要があります。必要事項を30語程度の英語で記入してみましょう。

Student Volunteer Application Form

We need student volunteers to help with the meeting and events for the Group Discussion Program that will be held in Vancouver, Canada, from August 4th to August 10th.　Please fill out the following form completely.

1. Name: _____　　2. High School: _____

3. Please write why you want to attend the meeting as a volunteer.

_____

_____

HINTS あなたが日本，アメリカ，メキシコ，南アフリカからの人々を迎えるつもりになって，国際交流の観点や異文化体験の観点から2文程度で書いてみましょう。

Helpful Expressions have a lot of opportunities to ～ 「～する機会がたくさんある」
introduce A to B 「BにAを紹介する」

本冊 Lesson 8 の英文をもう一度読んで，次の活動に取り組みましょう。

Words and Phrases 英文中に出てきた語句・表現について，それぞれ左側の空所には英語を，右側の空所には日本語の意味を書き入れましょう。

1. professor 名 [B1] _____

2. _____ 動 [A1] …を運営する

3. _____ 名 [A2] 目的

4. _____ 名 [A2] 機会

5. content 名 [B1] _____

6. agriculture 名 [B1] _____

7. climate change _____

8. extinction 名 [B1] _____

9. industry 名 [B1] _____

10. be willing to ～ _____

Questions 次の問いに英語で答えましょう。

1. According to the poster, what opportunity will high school students be offered in this event?

_____

2. What will the three professors talk about at the session?

_____

3. Who is probably a professor in the faculty of literature?

_____

4. What should the students prepare before giving a presentation at the lectures?

_____

Express Yourself あなたは英語でプレゼンテーションをします。そのタイトルを考え，要旨を30語程度の英語で紹介してみましょう。

My Presentation Title: _____

_____

_____

_____

HINTS I would like to talk about … など，プレゼンテーションを導入するフレーズを使い，そのまま実際のプレゼンテーションの冒頭で使えそうな英語を目指して書いてみましょう。

Helpful Expressions My presentation topic is … 「私のプレゼンテーションのトピックは…です」
environmental issues「環境問題」　international exchange「国際交流」　global warming「地球温暖化」

本冊 Lesson 9 の英文をもう一度読んで，次の活動に取り組みましょう。

Words and Phrases

英文中に出てきた語句・表現について，それぞれ左側の空所には英語を，右側の空所には日本語の意味を書き入れましょう。

1. instruction 名 [B1] ....
2. ingredient 名 [B1] ....
3. diameter 名 [B1] ....
4. put A into B ....
5. stir 動 [B1] ....

6. completely 副 [B1] ....
7. divide A into B ....
8. .... 動 [A2] …に達する
9. spread 動 [B2] ....
10. Why don't you 〜? ....

Questions

次の問いに英語で答えましょう。

1. If you follow the recipe, what will you make?

....

2. According to the recipe, how much olive oil do you need to make the dough?

....

3. According to the recipe, how long should you bake the pizzas in the oven?

....

4. What can you do after making pizzas with this recipe?

....

Express Yourself

次の空所に英語を補って，自分が作ることができる料理について簡単なレシピを作りましょう。

What Food Can You Make?

I can make ....

Ingredients: ....

Instructions

Step 1: ....

Step 2: ....

Step 3: ....

HINTS いくつかのものを列挙する場合は，A, B, C and D. のように表現しましょう。レシピの手順は命令文で書くことがポイント。

Helpful Expressions put ... together「…をいっしょにする」　heat ... in a pan「フライパンで温める[焼く]」
boil ... in a pot「なべでゆでる」　(thinly) slice ...「(肉・野菜・魚などを薄く)切る」

本冊 Lesson 10 の英文をもう一度読んで，次の活動に取り組みましょう。

Words and Phrases

英文中に出てきた語句・表現について，それぞれ左側の空所には英語を，右側の空所には日本語に意味を書き入れましょう。

1. examine 動 [B1] _____
2. _____ 動 [A2] …を説明する
3. _____ 名 [A2] 発音
4. informative 形 [B1] _____
5. thought-provoking 形 _____

6. _____ 名 [A2] 聴衆，観衆
7. fluent 形 [B1] _____
8. _____ 形 [A2] 全国的な
9. summarize 動 [B1] _____
10. determine 動 [B1] _____

Questions

次の問いに英語で答えましょう。

1. What did Yosuke talk about in his speech?

_____

2. Why was Yosuke's speech not received well by his audience?

_____

3. According to Mr. Green, how was Satsuki's speech?

_____

4. Which was more important for the judges, pronunciation or content, when a student was giving a speech?

_____

Express Yourself

あなたはウェブサイトに英語でレビューを投稿し，おすすめの商品を紹介します。あなたの気に入っている商品を紹介する文章を30語程度の英語で書いてみましょう。

Product: _____
Your Review ★★★★★ (5 stars)

_____
_____
_____

HINTS 本，服，靴，食べ物，飲み物，音楽，スマートフォンなど，自分の身の回りにあるもので考えてみましょう。また，実際に海外のショッピングサイトでレビューを見て，使われている英語表現を参考にしてみてもよいでしょう。

Helpful Expressions fantastic [wonderful / excellent] 「すばらしい」　　comfortable 「快適な」
delicious [tasty] 「おいしい（甘いものについては delicious を使うのがふつう）」
I recommend ... 「…をおすすめします」

本冊 Lesson 11 の英文をもう一度読んで，次の活動に取り組みましょう。

Words and Phrases 英文中に出てきた語句・表現について，それぞれ左側の空所には英語を，右側の空所には日本語の意味を書き入れましょう。

1. _____ 名 [A2] ディベート

2. _____ 名 [B1] ブログ

3. require 動 [B1] _____

4. _____ 形 [A2] 最近の

5. _____ 名 [A1] 調査

6. angle 名 [B1] _____

7. not ... at all _____

8. in one's view _____

9. _____ 動 [A2] 生き抜く

10. highly 副 [B1] _____

Questions 次の問いに英語で答えましょう。

1. According to the survey in paragraph 1, how does learning a foreign language help the learners?

_____

2. According to Tim, what do students understand by learning a foreign language?

_____

3. Why does Chloe believe that schools should not make the students study another language?

_____

4. What does the writer think about learning another language at school?

_____

Express Yourself 次のトピックについて，あなたは「賛成」の立場でディスカッションをします。書き出しに続けて，グラフを参考にしながら，あなたの意見を理由とともに30語程度の英語で書いてみましょう。

Statement It is bad for elementary school students to have their own SNS accounts.

I agree with this statement. _____

_____

子供が SNS を利用中にトラブルを経験したことがある

ある 26%

ない・その他 74%

HINTS 本冊 Lesson 11 の本文では a recent survey shows that ... や research suggests that ... など，調査・研究の結果を参照する表現が使われています。ここではグラフの内容を自分の意見の根拠として活用しましょう。

Helpful Expressions The graph shows that ... 「そのグラフは…ということを表す」
X% of the ... 「…の X パーセントが」
one in four children 「4人に1人の子供」

本冊 Lesson 12 の英文をもう一度読んで，次の活動に取り組みましょう。

Words and Phrases 英文中に出てきた語句・表現について，それぞれ左側の空所には英語を，右側の空所には日本語の意味を書き入れましょう。

1. tend to ~ ____
2. delicate 形 [B1] ____
3. ____ 名 [A2] 状況
4. ____ 名 [A1] おもちゃ
5. ____ 名 [A1] 部門
6. ____ 副 [A2] 主に
7. no longer ~ ____
8. separate 動 [B2] ____
9. freely 副 [B1] ____
10. in the future ____

Questions 次の問いに英語で答えましょう。

1. According to an article in the early 1900s, why was pink a color for boys?

2. According to the passage, what idea was introduced into choosing colors from the 1940s?

3. In which color section did people probably find radio-controlled robots?

4. Why do some toy stores in Europe and the U.S. no longer separate toys into a boys' section and a girls' section?

Express Yourself 次の質問について，あなたの考えとその理由を30語程度の英語で書いてみましょう。

Question: Do you think it is a good idea for children to choose their toys by themselves?

HINTS まずは，質問に対する自分の立場を明確にしましょう。子供が自分でおもちゃを選ぶことのメリットとデメリットを考えて，自分の考えをまとめてみましょう。

Helpful Expressions make one's own choice「自分で選択をする」 respect one's personality「個性を尊重する」 toys which are bad for one's education「教育に悪いおもちゃ」

本冊 Lesson 13 の英文をもう一度読んで，次の活動に取り組みましょう。

Words and Phrases
英文中に出てきた語句・表現について，それぞれ左側の空所には英語を，右側の空所には日本語の意味を書き入れましょう。

1. _____ 图 [A2] 本棚
2. by oneself _____
3. assemble 動 [B2] _____
4. a wide variety of ... _____
5. recommend 動 [B1] _____

6. _____ 图 [A2] 初心者
7. put up ... _____
8. attach 動 [B1] _____
9. fix 動 [B1] _____
10. height 图 [B1] _____

Questions
次の問いに英語で答えましょう。

1. According to the instructions, where should we put four of the wood dowels?

_____

2. When do we use a hammer?

_____

3. How do we hold up the two middle shelves?

_____

4. How do we put the middle shelves at different heights?

_____

Express Yourself
自動販売機での飲み物の買い方を海外からの観光客に説明する英語を書いてみましょう。

How to Use a Vending Machine
Step 1: _____
Step 2: _____
Step 3: _____
Step 4: _____

HINTS 例えば，次のような日本語を参考にして，自動販売機での飲み物の買い方について考えてみましょう。
Step 1：どの飲み物を買うか選ぶ。 → Step 2：自動販売機にお金を入れる。 → Step 3：ボタンを押す。 → Step 4：自動販売機から飲み物を取り出す。
本文同様に，それぞれの手順は命令形で説明しましょう。

Helpful Expressions a vending machine「自動販売機」　put money into ...「…へお金を入れる」
take out A from B「AをBから取り出す」

本冊 Lesson 14 の英文をもう一度読んで，次の活動に取り組みましょう。

Words and Phrases 英文中に出てきた語句・表現について，それぞれ左側の空所には英語を，右側の空所には日本語の意味を書き入れましょう。

1. _____ 名 [A2] 制服

2. not ～ without ... _____

3. _____ 動 [A2] …を含む

4. _____ 名 [A2] 外見

5. for one's age _____

6. be used to ～ing _____

7. _____ 動 [A1] …を判断する

8. _____ 名 [A2] 社会

9. obey 動 [B2] _____

10. _____ 名 [A2] 法律

Questions 次の問いに英語で答えましょう。

1. What was Sarah surprised at when she visited a high school in Osaka?

_____

2. According to the article, what should the students wear at school every day?

_____

3. If a student is late for school five times, what must he or she do?

_____

4. What does Alastair think about Japanese school rules, and why?

_____

Express Yourself 新しい校則を作るとしたらどのようなものがよいでしょうか。理由とともに合計30語程度の英語で書いてみましょう。

A New School Rule

You should _____

Reason

_____

_____

HINTS 新しい校則は何かを禁止することだけではなく，生徒のためになることや身を守ること，またはユニークな校則について考えてみてもよいでしょう。

例：防犯ブザー（a safety alarm）を身につけること，1日に1回は英語を話すこと，月に1回は自分の好きな服装で登校することなど。

本冊 Lesson 15 の英文をもう一度読んで，次の活動に取り組みましょう。

Words and Phrases 英文中に出てきた語句・表現について，それぞれ左側の空所には英語を，右側の空所には日本語の意味を書き入れましょう。

1. career 名 [B1] ＿＿＿＿＿＿＿
2. ＿＿＿＿＿＿＿ 名 [A1] 週末
3. ＿＿＿＿＿＿＿ 名 [A1] 祖父[母]
4. roast 形 [B2] ＿＿＿＿＿＿＿
5. architect 名 [B1] ＿＿＿＿＿＿＿

6. ＿＿＿＿＿＿＿ 名 [A2] 経験
7. ＿＿＿＿＿＿＿ 形 [A2] 役立つ
8. ＿＿＿＿＿＿＿ 名 [A2] 編集者
9. ＿＿＿＿＿＿＿ 名 [A2] 弁護士
10. make a speech ＿＿＿＿＿＿＿

Questions 次の問いに英語で答えましょう。

1. According to the e-mail, what did Barry like very much at the Sunday lunch?

＿＿＿＿＿＿＿＿＿＿＿＿＿＿＿＿＿＿＿＿＿＿＿＿＿＿＿＿＿＿

2. Who are Barry's teachers looking for?

＿＿＿＿＿＿＿＿＿＿＿＿＿＿＿＿＿＿＿＿＿＿＿＿＿＿＿＿＿＿

3. What is Diana's job?

＿＿＿＿＿＿＿＿＿＿＿＿＿＿＿＿＿＿＿＿＿＿＿＿＿＿＿＿＿＿

4. What does Barry ask Diana to do next month?

＿＿＿＿＿＿＿＿＿＿＿＿＿＿＿＿＿＿＿＿＿＿＿＿＿＿＿＿＿＿

Express Yourself あなたは来月に中学校の同窓会を開こうと思います。中学校の恩師の先生に同窓会への出席をお願いするメールを，30語程度の英語で書いてみましょう。

Subject: Junior High School Class Reunion

From: ＿＿＿＿＿＿＿＿＿＿＿＿＿＿

To: ＿＿＿＿＿＿＿＿＿＿＿＿＿＿

＿＿＿＿＿＿＿＿＿＿＿＿＿＿＿＿＿＿＿＿＿＿＿＿＿＿＿＿＿＿＿＿

＿＿＿＿＿＿＿＿＿＿＿＿＿＿＿＿＿＿＿＿＿＿＿＿＿＿＿＿＿＿＿＿

＿＿＿＿＿＿＿＿＿＿＿＿＿＿＿＿＿＿＿＿＿＿＿＿＿＿＿＿＿＿＿＿

HINTS Lesson 15 のメール本文にある"How are you doing?"といったあいさつ文や，"Can I ask you a favor?"や"Would you come to ...?"といった依頼をする文を参考にしましょう。

Helpful Expressions a class reunion「同窓会」 hold「…を開催する」 please let me know「お知らせください」

本冊 Lesson 16 の英文をもう一度読んで，次の活動に取り組みましょう。

Words and Phrases 英文中に出てきた語句・表現について，それぞれ左側の空所には英語を，右側の空所には日本語の意味を書き入れましょう。

1. the other day   ----------------------

2. ---------------------- 图 [A1] 屋台

3. surprisingly 副 [B1] ----------------------

4. ---------------------- 副 [A1] すばやく

5. ---------------------- 形 [A2] 伝統的な

6. look like ...   ----------------------

7. hesitate to ～   ----------------------

8. firework 图 [B1]   ----------------------

9. ---------------------- 動 [A2] …に感銘を与える

10. ---------------------- 動 [A2] …を期待する

Questions 次の問いに英語で答えましょう。

1. Who took the writer of this article to a Japanese summer festival?

----

2. What did the writer eat at the festival?

----

3. Why couldn't the writer get any goldfish at all?

----

4. What did the writer buy and where did she buy it before seeing the fireworks?

Express Yourself 日本の夏祭りで，海外から訪れた人にいちばん見てほしいもの，またはやってみてほしいことを，理由とともに30語程度の英語で紹介してみましょう。

What you should see and do at a Japanese summer festival:

HINTS 日本の夏祭りで海外からの訪問者にもよく知られている風物詩には，「花火」「盆踊り」「屋台」「縁日のゲーム」「浴衣」などがあります。これらについて考えてみるとよいでしょう。

本冊 Lesson 17 の英文をもう一度読んで，次の活動に取り組みましょう。

Words and Phrases 英文中に出てきた語句・表現について，それぞれ左側の空所には英語を，右側の空所には日本語の意味を書き入れましょう。

1. _____ 名 [A1] 島

2. to the north of ... _____

3. _____ 名 [A2] 風景

4. as if ... _____

5. float 動 [B1] _____

6. give up ～ing _____

7. _____ 動 [A2] 賃借りする

8. scenic 形 [B1] _____

9. get lost _____

10. _____ 副 [A2] いつか

Questions 次の問いに英語で答えましょう。

1. Where is Melony Island located?

_____

2. What did the writer enjoy on the train to the island?

_____

3. What did the couple do on the afternoon of the second day?

_____

4. How did the couple go around the island on the last day?

_____

Express Yourself あなたは旅行に出かけようと考えています。旅行先を自分で決め，旅行の予定を30語程度の英語で書いてみましょう。

My Travel Plan for _____

_____

_____

_____

HINTS 観光地を見てまわること，海水浴やスキーなどのスポーツをすること，地元のおいしい料理を食べることなどがあります。予定を書くときには，in the morning や after that などの時間的順序を表す表現を使いましょう。

Helpful Expressions sightseeing spots「観光地」 see the sights of ...「…を観光する」 local food「地元の料理」

本冊 Lesson 18 の英文をもう一度読んで，次の活動に取り組みましょう。

Words and Phrases 英文中に出てきた語句・表現について，それぞれ左側の空所には英語を，右側の空所には日本語の意味を書き入れましょう。

1. have an interest in ... _____
2. separately 副 [B2] _____
3. _____ 名 [A1] 活動
4. have ... in common _____
5. _____ 副 [A2] ついに

6. _____ 名 [A2] 性格
7. immediately 副 [B1] _____
8. to one's surprise _____
9. _____ 名 [A1] 妻
10. characteristic 名 [B1] _____

Questions 次の問いに英語で答えましょう。

1. What kind of interest do scientists have in twins?

_____

2. In the second paragraph, how many questions were the two pairs of twins asked?

_____

3. What was the most interesting to the writer?

_____

4. What were one pair of twins who met after 40 years apart surprised at?

_____

_____

Express Yourself あなたの好きな [得意な] 教科を 3 つ挙げ，その理由を英語で書きましょう。

Subject ① _____

_____

Subject ② _____

_____

Subject ③ _____

_____

HINTS 理由は「興味があること」や，「ふだん自分がやっていること（英語のリスニングを毎日やっているなど）」など，いろいろなことが考えられます。

Helpful Expressions be good at ... 「…が得意だ」　　it is interesting for me to 〜 「私は〜をするのがおもしろい」

Lesson 19

本冊 Lesson 19 の英文をもう一度読んで，次の活動に取り組みましょう。

Words and Phrases 英文中に出てきた語句・表現について，それぞれ左側の空所には英語を，右側の空所には日本語の意味を書き入れましょう。

1. be familiar with ... _____
2. typical 形 [B1] _____
3. _____ 副 [A2] おそらく
4. properly 副 [B1] _____
5. _____ 動 [A2] …に入る

6. wipe 動 [B2] _____
7. so that ... can ～ _____
8. _____ 形 [A1] 失礼な
9. be content with ... _____
10. avoid ～ing _____

Questions 次の問いに英語で答えましょう。

1. According to the article, what is a wet towel used for in a Japanese restaurant?

_____

2. Why shouldn't we make a noise while eating in the U.S.?

_____

3. Why should we make a sipping sound when we drink a cup of green tea at the end of a tea ceremony?

_____

4. Why should we avoid holding food with two pairs of chopsticks?

_____

Express Yourself 海外の人に紹介したい日本の食事のマナーを，30語程度の英語で説明してみましょう。

_____
_____
_____

HINTS 「いただきます」や「ごちそうさま」の挨拶などを思い浮かべてみましょう。「座る場所」，「食べる順序」，「魚の食べ方」など，意外と知らない日本の食事のルールはたくさんあります。どのようなものがあるか自分で調べてみるとよいでしょう。

Helpful Expressions it is not a good idea to ～「～するのはよくない考えだ（～しないほうがよい）」
it is polite to ～「～すると礼儀正しい」

本冊 Lesson 20 の英文をもう一度読んで，次の活動に取り組みましょう。

Words and Phrases
英文中に出てきた語句・表現について，それぞれ左側の空所には英語を，右側の空所には日本語の意味を書き入れましょう。

1. damage 動 [B1] _____

2. environment 名 [B2] _____

3. _____ 名 [A2] 製品

4. years ago _____

5. protect 動 [B1] _____

6. project 名 [B2] _____

7. _____ 名 [A2] 影響（力）

8. not only A but also B _____

9. see the sights _____

10. _____ 前 [A2] …を除いて

Questions
次の問いに英語で答えましょう。

1. According to the passage, what do we recycle in order not to damage the environment?

_____

2. How many purposes of ecotourism are listed in the passage?

_____

3. Why is it important to learn about the culture and history of the place that we are going to visit?

_____

4. What will happen if we use the local language with the local people?

_____

Express Yourself
あなたはニュージーランド旅行中に行うアクティビティを選んでいます。次の2つから自分が予約したいものを選び，その理由を30語程度の英語で書いてみましょう。

_____

_____

_____

1. Ship Cruise from Queenstown	2. Dolphin Tour in Kaikoura
Discover the beauty of the Fiordland National Park and Milford Sound from a Queenstown day trip.	This trip offers the opportunity to watch or even swim with wild dolphins.

HINTS I would like to reserve ... 「…を予約したいです」から文を始めて，どんなことを楽しみにしているかを書くとよいでしょう。フィヨルドランド国立公園やミルフォードサウンド，カイコウラなどは，イメージをつかむためにインターネットなどで調べてみてもよいでしょう。

Helpful Expressions reserve [book] 「(ホテル，チケット，ツアーなど)を予約する」
look forward to ～ing 「～することを楽しみにする」

本冊 Lesson 21 の英文をもう一度読んで，次の活動に取り組みましょう。

Words and Phrases　英文中に出てきた語句・表現について，それぞれ左側の空所には英語を，右側の空所には日本語の意味を書き入れましょう。

1. ＿＿＿＿＿＿＿＿＿　動 [A2] 卒業する

2. ＿＿＿＿＿＿＿＿＿　動 [A2] 演奏する

3. rare 形 [B1]　＿＿＿＿＿＿＿＿＿

4. ＿＿＿＿＿＿＿＿＿　形 [A1] にぎやかな

5. impression 名 [B1]　＿＿＿＿＿＿＿＿＿

6. this is because ...　＿＿＿＿＿＿＿＿＿

7. have an impact on ...　＿＿＿＿＿＿＿＿＿

8. ＿＿＿＿＿＿＿＿＿　動 [A2] …を創造する

9. in the past　＿＿＿＿＿＿＿＿＿

10. even if ...　＿＿＿＿＿＿＿＿＿

Questions　次の問いに英語で答えましょう。

1. According to the passage, what did the writer do after his graduation from university?

＿＿＿＿＿＿＿＿＿＿＿＿＿＿＿＿＿＿＿＿＿＿＿＿＿＿＿＿＿＿

2. How long did the writer work in New York?

＿＿＿＿＿＿＿＿＿＿＿＿＿＿＿＿＿＿＿＿＿＿＿＿＿＿＿＿＿＿

3. What was the writer's first impression of Tokyo?

＿＿＿＿＿＿＿＿＿＿＿＿＿＿＿＿＿＿＿＿＿＿＿＿＿＿＿＿＿＿

4. How does the writer compose music now?

＿＿＿＿＿＿＿＿＿＿＿＿＿＿＿＿＿＿＿＿＿＿＿＿＿＿＿＿＿＿

Express Yourself　あなたは高校を卒業した後にどんなことをしたいですか。卒業後のあなたの状況を自由に想像して，30語程度の英語で書いてみましょう。

＿＿＿＿＿＿＿＿＿＿＿＿＿＿＿＿＿＿＿＿＿＿＿＿＿＿＿＿＿＿

＿＿＿＿＿＿＿＿＿＿＿＿＿＿＿＿＿＿＿＿＿＿＿＿＿＿＿＿＿＿

＿＿＿＿＿＿＿＿＿＿＿＿＿＿＿＿＿＿＿＿＿＿＿＿＿＿＿＿＿＿

[HINTS] 将来の夢のために大学で何を学びたいかや，技術習得のために海外に留学する姿などを思い描きながら書いてみましょう。

[Helpful Expressions] would like to ～「～したい」　　work as ...「…として働く」　　in the future「将来」

本冊 Lesson 22 の英文をもう一度読んで，次の活動に取り組みましょう。

Words and Phrases

英文中に出てきた語句・表現について，それぞれ左側の空所には英語を，右側の空所には日本語の意味を書き入れましょう。

1. journalist 名 [B1] ....

2. more and more ... .

3. design 動 [B1] ....

4. device 名 [B1] ....

5. .... 名 [A2] 現金

6. .... 動 [A2] …のままである

7. secure 形 [B1] ....

8. run out ....

9. depend on ... .

10. .... 副 [A2] もしかしたら

Questions

次の問いに英語で答えましょう。

1. According to the passage, where can we put our mobile wallets?

....

2. What should we do before we start to use mobile wallets?

....

3. Why can we pay faster if we use mobile wallets?

....

4. Why do people possibly spend too much money if they use mobile wallets?

....

Express Yourself

次の棒グラフは，日本の電子マネーの決済件数の推移を表したものです。このグラフが表す内容を30語程度の英語で説明してみましょう。

....

....

....

電子マネーの決済件数
(百万件)
7,000
6,000 5,853
5,000
4,000
3,000 2,720
2,000
1,000
0
2012年 2018年

HINTS 「電子マネーの決済件数」は the number of electronic money payments と表します。グラフからどのような傾向が読み取れるかを説明してみましょう。

Helpful Expressions
increase by about 3 billion 「約30億件増加する」
more and more people ～ 「ますます多くの人が～する」
the number of ... 「…の数」
the number almost doubled 「その数はほぼ倍増した」

解答・解説

Lesson 1

Words and Phrases

1. ～しようとしている　　2. …に向けて出発する
3. 留学する　　4. flight　　5. somewhere
6. actually　　7. …を見回す　　8. carefully
9. instead　　10. 必ず

Questions

1. He is at Kansai International Airport.

解説 At Kansai International Airport. だけでもよいが，主語＋動詞の形で答えたい。朗太の最初のメッセージ I am at Kansai International Airport. がポイント。

2. He needs his passport and boarding pass.

解説 質問文は「朗太のフライトに必要なもの」をたずねている。本文の I need them by 4 p.m. today to be in time for my flight. の them は「朗太のパスポートと搭乗券」を指す。

3. They are in his travel bag.

解説 質問文は「朗太のパスポートと搭乗券はどこにあるか」である。これは朗太の兄が Routa, actually, your passport and boarding pass should be in your travel bag. と言っており，その返事として朗太が Yes, I found my passport and boarding pass! と言っているのが解答のポイント。

4. He left his tablet PC there.

解説 質問文は「朗太は家に何を忘れたか」である。兄からのメッセージの Instead, I have found your tablet PC. から，忘れたと思っていたパスポートと搭乗券ではなく，タブレットパソコンを忘れているとわかる。

Express Yourself

例：I'm so happy to receive my tablet PC. Thank you for sending it! How are you doing? I'm enjoying my life in New York. I have already made friends with my classmates. They are from various countries. （37 words）

和訳 タブレット PC を受け取ってとてもうれしいよ。送ってくれてありがとう！　元気にしてる？　僕はニューヨークでの生活を楽しんでいるよ。クラスメートとはもう友達になったよ。彼らはさまざまな国から来ているんだ。

Lesson 2

Words and Phrases

1. すばらしい，驚くべき　　2. …で有名だ
3. 独特の　　4. national　　5. unusual
6. every　　7. AからBまで　　8. ticket
9. …を探す　　10. 宿泊設備

Questions

1. We can watch unique animals there.

解説 質問文は「オーストラリアで何を見ることができるか」である。第1段落1文目に「オーストラリアは，ほかにはない独特な動物を見るのにすばらしい場所であることで有名」とある。

2. It has some unusual animals, such as crocodiles, colorful wild birds, and Australian frogs.

解説 質問文は「デインツリー国立公園にはどんな動物がいるか」である。第1段落3文目にその具体例が示されている。

3. We can buy one at the information center.

解説 質問文は「バスツアーのチケットをどこで購入できるか」をたずねている。本文の第2段落2文目がポイント。a tour bus ticket は不特定のものなので，it ではなく不定代名詞 one で受けることに注意。

4. It will cost $50.

解説 質問文は「大人2人，10歳の子供1人のチケットを購入する場合，いくらかかるか」である。本文の Ticket Prices の大人20ドル，3歳から14歳の子供10ドルという記述から計算して答えを求める。

Express Yourself

例：① where can I buy　　② How much are they?　　③ can I buy two adult tickets and two child tickets

和訳 あなた：すみません。一日券をどこで買うことができますか。

スタッフ：ここで買えますよ。

あなた：いくらでしょうか。

スタッフ：大人1人15ドル，3歳以上の子供は1人8ドルです。3歳未満の子供にはチケットは必要ありません。

あなた：ありがとうございます。それなら，大人2枚，子供2枚のチケットをいただけますか。

スタッフ：わかりました。それでは4名様で46ドルになります。

あなた：ありがとう！

Lesson 3

Words and Phrases

1. …のようだ　　2. 合計の　　3. 多くても
4. 研究者　　5. 少なくとも　　6. therefore
7. ～することにおいて　　8. できるだけ…
9. ～するのに…を費やす　　10. …が上達する

Questions

1. Yes, they do.

解説 質問文は「本文によれば，日本のすべての中学生と高校生は，学校で英語を勉強しなくてはな

らない」である。本文2文目を読むと，答えは Yes であることがわかる。

2. They need at least about 3,000 hours.

解説 質問文は「一部の研究者によれば，学習者が英語を習得するのに何時間必要とするか」である。本文の4文目を参考に答える。

3. To use [Using] it as often as possible outside of school is.

解説 質問文は「英語学習において大切なことは何か」である。本文の第5文に答えがある。What is ...? でたずねられているので，to- 不定詞や動名詞を使って「できるだけ頻繁に学校外で英語を使うこと」という名詞句を作る。

4. We will get better at it.

解説 質問文は「英語を使うことにより多くの時間を費やすと，何が起こるか」である。本文の最終文を参考に答える。

Express Yourself

例：A good way to learn English is to read English comic books. We can enjoy reading them and learn various English words and phrases at the same time. (28 words)

和訳 英語を学ぶよい方法は，英語の漫画を読むことです。私たちはそれらを読んで楽しむと同時に，さまざまな英語の単語やフレーズを学ぶことができます。

Lesson 4

Words and Phrases

1. order　　2. ～してくれてありがとう
3. unfortunately　　4. online　　5. instead
6. 味　　7. 香り　　8. …を取り消す
9. …するように手配する　　10. …を指定する

Questions

1. Because the company sells it only in the U.K.

解説 質問文は「メールによると，なぜマリエはオレンジティーを手に入れることができないのか」である。第1段落の2文目に注目すると，この会社はマリエが注文したオレンジティーをイギリスでのみ販売しているとある。

2. It can send lemon tea to her.

解説 質問文は「その会社はオレンジティーの代わりにマリエに何を送ることができるか」である。この答えは第1段落3文目にある。

3. Because its taste and fragrance are as good as those of the orange tea.

解説 質問文は「なぜその会社はマリエがレモンティーを気に入ると思っているのか」である。その理由として，第1段落4文目に，レモンティーの味や香りが，マリエが注文したオレンジティーと

同等であることが挙げられている。

4. She should tell it when she needs it by and how much tea she needs.

解説 質問文は「マリエがレモンティーを注文する場合，彼女は何を会社に伝えるべきか」である。第2段落で，「いつまでに必要か」と「どれくらい必要か」という2点が挙げられており，それらを答える。

Express Yourself

例：Thank you for e-mailing me. I would like to order the lemon tea instead of the orange tea. Could you send me 100 grams of the lemon tea? I need it by October 25th. (34 words)

和訳 メールをいただき，ありがとうございます。オレンジティーの代わりにレモンティーを注文したいと思います。私に100gのレモンティーを送っていただけますか。私は10月25日までにそれが必要です。

Lesson 5

Words and Phrases

1. theater　　2. each　　3. 前もって
4. アイコン　　5. 入手できる　　6. …に進む
7. 購入　　8. without　　9. 並んで待つ
10. strange

Questions

1. It means no seats are available for that showtime.

解説 質問文は「カレンダーに顔のアイコンが表示されたら，何を意味するか」である。Ticket Finder の3文目が答えのポイント。

2. It is "Strange Adventure."

解説 質問文は「ウェブサイト上の表によると，ファンタジー映画の題名は何か」である。表中でファンタジー映画は『ストレンジアドベンチャー』のみなので，これが答えだとわかる。

3. "Fantastic Phoenix" is.

解説 質問文は「3つの中で上映時間がいちばん長い映画はどれか」である。上映時間が3時間20分の『ファンタスティックフェニックス』が3つの中で最長である。

4. Only adults aged 18 or older can.

解説 質問文は「だれが夜間上映を見ることができるか」である。本文の終わりに夜間上映についての条件が記述されている。

Express Yourself

例：My favorite movie is "The Avengers." This is an American superhero film. I like American culture, so I can fully enjoy this movie from a cultural point of view. (29 words)

和訳 私の好きな映画は『アベンジャーズ』です。これはアメリカのスーパーヒーロー映画です。私はアメリカ文化が好きなので，この映画を文化的な観点から存分に楽しむことができます。

Lesson 6

Words and Phrases
1. flight 　 2. …を楽しみに待つ
3. vacation 　 4. local 　 5. …を迎えに行く
6. airport 　 7. お安いごようです 　 8. relax
9. …を起こす 　 10. difference

Questions
1. He wants him to pick him up at the airport.

解説 質問文は「ロバートはフランクに何をしてほしいか」をたずねている。1通目のメールのCould you do me a favor? 以降から，何をお願いしているかを読み取る。

2. It takes about three hours.

解説 質問文は「フランクの家から空港まで車でどれくらいかかるか」をたずねている。これは2通目のメールの It takes ... 以下に答えがある。

3. He will drink coffee and read some books.

解説 質問文は「ロバートはフランクを待っている間，何をするか」をたずねている。3通目のメールの3文目に答えがある。

4. He probably lives in Japan.

解説 質問文は「ロバートはおそらくどの国に住んでいるか」をたずねている。これは3通目のメールの5文目の情報から推測して考える。6:30 a.m. in Los Angeles is 11:30 p.m. in my country, Japan. で，Japan を my country としている。

Express Yourself
例：I prefer traveling by train because I can enjoy the view from the train. Also, I can get on the train soon after it gets into the station. (28 words)

別解：I prefer traveling by plane because it is much faster than traveling by train. I can save time, and I can stay longer at my destination. (26 words)

和訳 私は列車での旅行が好きです。なぜなら列車からの景色を楽しむことができるからです。また，列車が駅に入ってきてすぐ乗ることができるからです。

別解：列車で移動するよりもずっと速いので，私は飛行機で旅行することが好きです。時間を節約することができ，目的地でより長く滞在することができます。

Lesson 7

Words and Phrases
1. notice 　 2. 毎年の 　 3. 参加者
4. ～するために(目的を表す) 　 5. …に加えて
6. manage 　 7. 別れ 　 8. basic 　 9. apply
10. …に必要事項を記入する

Questions
1. It will be held in Vancouver, Canada.

解説 質問文は「どこでグループディスカッションプログラムが開催されるか」と「場所」をたずねている。

2. One hundred people will.

解説 「日本から何人の人がグループディスカッションプログラムに参加するか」と「人数」をたずねている。

3. They will give them on August 6th.

解説 「いつ地球温暖化に関するプレゼンテーションをするのか」という「時」をたずねている。

4. Discussions and presentations will.

解説 「カンファレンスセンターで何が行われるか」をたずねている。答えは複数形となる点に注意。

Express Yourself
例：3. By attending this meeting as a volunteer, I will have a lot of opportunities to learn about different cultures and values. Also, I would like to introduce the unique culture of Canada to the participants. (35 words)

和訳 この会合にボランティアとして参加することで，私はさまざまな文化や価値観を学ぶ多くの機会を得るでしょう。また，私は参加者にカナダ独特の文化を紹介したいと思っています。

Lesson 8

Words and Phrases
1. 教授 　 2. run 　 3. purpose 　 4. opportunity
5. 内容 　 6. 農業 　 7. 気候変動 　 8. 絶滅
9. 産業 　 10. 快く～する

Questions
1. They will be offered an opportunity to meet university professors and learn more about what is taught at the university.

解説 質問文は「このイベントで高校生はどんな機会が与えられるか」である。ポスター上部にあるイベント説明の中の The purpose of this event is to ～ に，このイベントの目的が述べられており，高校生ができることは「大学教授に会って，大学で教えられている内容をより知る」ことである。

2. They will talk about their own research fields.

解説 質問文は「そのセッションで3人の教授は何

について話すか」である。星の光サマーセッションの Event の箇所に注目する。そこに「それぞれの研究分野について話をする」とあるので，これを参考にして答えるとよい。

3. Yoko Collins is.

解説 質問文は「だれが文学部の教授だと推測されるか」である。ポスター中に明確には示されていないが，各教授の研究分野の内容から文学部で教えていそうな教授を推測する。

4. They should prepare slides with photos.

解説 質問文は「生徒は講義でプレゼンテーションをする前に何を準備すべきか」である。本文の最終部分の「写真付きのスライドを用意してください」が答えのポイント。

Express Yourself

例：The Tourism Industry in Japan
I would like to talk about the tourism industry in Japan. Recently, more and more people from other countries are visiting Japan. Japanese food culture and the history of Japan are popular among them. （34 words）

和訳 私は日本の観光産業について話したいと思います。最近は，海外からますます多くの人々が日本を訪れています。日本の食文化と歴史が外国人の間で人気があります。

Lesson 9

Words and Phrases

1. 指示，説明　　2. 材料　　3. 直径
4. AをBの中に入れる　　5. …をかき混ぜる
6. 完全に　　7. AをBに分ける　　8. reach
9. …を広げる　　10. ～してはどうですか

Questions

1. We will make two pizzas for about four people.

解説 質問文は「レシピに従うと何ができるか」をたずねている。本文の Ingredients に続く箇所を参考にするとよい。

2. We need two tablespoons of it.

解説 質問文は「生地を作るのにオリーブオイルがどのくらい必要か」をたずねている。two tablespoons of ... 「大さじ2杯の…」という表現を使えるとよい。

3. We should bake them for about 10 minutes.

解説 質問文は「ピザを何分焼くか」をたずねている。本文の Step 2 の 2. Put the pizzas into the oven and ... を参考にして答えを作る。

4. We can take pictures of our pizzas and post them on SNSs.

解説 質問文は「このレシピでピザを作った後，何

ができるか」である。本文の最後にある If you use this recipe, why don't you ...? を参考にして答えを作るとよい。

Express Yourself

例・和訳

I can make pancakes with a lot of honey. （ハチミツたっぷりのホットケーキが作れます。）

Ingredients: Pancake mix, milk, butter and an egg. （ホットケーキミックス，牛乳，バター，卵。）

Step 1: Put the pancake mix, milk and egg together and mix them. （ホットケーキミックス，牛乳そして卵をいっしょにして，混ぜる。）

Step 2: Heat the mixture with butter in a pan. （混ぜたものをフライパンでバターで焼く。）

Step 3: Serve the pancakes with a lot of honey. （パンケーキをたっぷりのハチミツといっしょに出す。）

Lesson 10

Words and Phrases

1. …を調べる　　2. explain　　3. pronunciation
4. 有益な，情報に富む　　5. 示唆に富む
6. audience　　7. 流ちょうな　　8. national
9. …を要約する　　10. …を決定する

Questions

1. He talked about one of his personal experiences.

解説 質問文は「陽介は彼のスピーチで何について話したか」である。ローズ先生のコメントに，His main topic was one of his personal experiences. とある。

2. Because he didn't make good eye-contact with his audience.

解説 質問文は「なぜ陽介のスピーチは聴衆にうまく伝わらなかったか」である。ローズ先生のコメントの3文目の However, since he didn't make good eye-contact with his audience, ... を参考に答えを作る。

3. Her speech was (not only) fluent and sounded really natural (but also it was really unique and most of the audience found it interesting).

解説 質問文は「グリーン先生のコメントによれば，沙月のスピーチはどうだったか」である。コメント後半の Not only that, her story was really unique and most of the audience found it interesting. の部分を解答に含めてもよい。

4. Pronunciation was.

解説 質問文は「審査員にとっては，生徒がスピーチを行う際に発音と内容のどちらのほうが大切だったか」である。Judges' shared evaluation の2文目に，We, the judges, have agreed that the pronunciation of the speech is more important than the content ... とある。

Express Yourself

例：Chocolate Crunch Bar
I really like this chocolate bar. It soon melts in my mouth and I can enjoy the chocolate flavor very much. I really recommend that you should buy one. (29 words)

和訳 私はこのチョコレートバーが大好きです。それは口の中ですぐに溶けて，チョコレートの香りを楽しむことができます。1つ買うことを本当におすすめします。

Lesson 11

Words and Phrases

1. debate　　2. blog　　3. …を要求する
4. recent　　5. survey　　6. 角度
7. 決して…ない　　8. …の考えでは　　9. survive
10. 非常に，高度に

Questions

1. It helps them see things from different angles.

解説 質問文は「第1段落の調査によると，別の言語を学ぶことはその学習者にどのように役に立つのか」である。第1段落2文目に「ものごとをいろいろな角度から見るのに役立つ」とある。

2. They understand the importance of respecting people with different values.

解説 質問文は「ティムによると，外国語を学習することで生徒はどのようなことを理解するようになるか」である。ティムの投稿の2文目に注目する。

3. Because learning a foreign language may be too difficult for some students.

別解：Because knowing a foreign language is not useful for some students.

解説 質問文は「なぜクロエは学校が生徒たちに別の言語を無理やり学ばせるべきではないと思っているか」である。クロエの投稿に2つの意見が述べられており，そのどちらかを解答する。

4. The writer thinks it is necessary in order to survive in this highly globalized world.

解説 質問文は「筆者は別の言語を学ぶことについてどのように思っているか」である。これは最終段落2文目に注目する。本文の learning another language を it で受けて，答えをまとめる。

Express Yourself

例：The graph shows that one in four children have had problems when using SNSs. I think that, in order to avoid such problems, elementary school students should not have their own SNS accounts. (33 words)

和訳 グラフは，4人に1人の子供がSNSのトラブルを経験したことがあると表しています。私は，このようなトラブルを避けるために，小学生はSNSのアカウントを持つべきではないと思います。

Lesson 12

Words and Phrases

1. ～する傾向がある　　2. 優美な　　3. situation
4. toy　　5. section　　6. mainly　　7. もう～ない
8. …を分ける　　9. 自由に　　10. 将来

Questions

1. Because it was seen as a strong color.

解説 質問文は「1900年代初頭の記事によれば，なぜピンクは男の子の色だったのか」である。本文の第1段落3文目に注目する。The reason is that pink was seen as a strong color ... が答えの根拠となる。

2. The idea that girls should be as strong as boys and boys should be more kind to others was.

解説 質問文は「1940年代から，どのような考えが色の選択に導入されたか」である。これは「女の子が強くあるべきで，男の子が他人により親切にすべきだという考え」ということが書かれている，第2段落2文目に注目する。

3. They probably found them in the blue section.

解説 質問文は「ラジコンロボットはおそらくどちらのセクションで見つかったか」である。第2段落の内容から，男の子向けのおもちゃは青いセクションにあったことがわかる。

4. Because they feel that children should freely choose what they want to play with and learn a lot of things from it.

解説 質問文は「なぜヨーロッパとアメリカの一部の玩具店はおもちゃをもう男の子と女の子のセクションに分けないのか」である。第3段落3文目に注目する。

Express Yourself

例：Yes, I do. I believe children who can make their own decisions will grow up to be adults who can respect the choices of others in the future. (28 words)

別解：No, I don't. If they can choose their toys freely, they may choose something bad for their education. In order to avoid that, their parents should choose their toys for them. (31 words)

和訳 はい，私はそう思います。私は，自分で選ぶことのできる子供は，将来他者の選択を尊重できる大人に育つと信じています。

別解：いいえ，そうは思いません。彼らが自由にお

もちゃを選ぶことができたら，彼らは教育によく
ないものを選ぶかもしれません。それを避けるた
めにも，親が彼らのためにおもちゃを選んであげ
るべきです。

Lesson 13
Words and Phrases
1. bookshelf　　2. ひとりで　　3. …を組み立てる
4. さまざまな種類の…　　　　5. …をすすめる
6. beginner　　7. …を組み立てる
8. …をつける　　9. …を固定する　　10. 高さ

Questions
1. We should put them into the holes of one side panel.

解説 質問文は「木製ダボ4本をどこに入れるか」
である。本文の Step 2 の1文目に注目する。

2. We use it when we put two nails into the top board and two nails into the bottom board.

解説 質問文は「いつハンマーを使うか」である。
Step 3 の2文目にハンマーを使う場面の記述が
ある。

3. We use eight metal pins to do that.

解説 質問文は「どのように中の2つの棚を支える
か」である。Step 4 の1文目を参考にする。

4. We move the metal pins into other holes to do that.

解説 質問文は「どのようにして中板を違う高さに
置くか」である。中板を支えている金属ピンの場
所を変えることで，中板の高さを変えることがで
きることが Step 4 の2文目に書かれている。

Express Yourself
例・和訳

Step 1: Choose which drink you want to buy.
（買いたい飲み物を選ぶ。）

Step 2: Put money into the vending machine.
（自動販売機にお金を入れる。）

Step 3: Push the button for the drink you want.
（買いたい飲み物のボタンを押す。）

Step 4: Take out the drink from the vending machine.（自動販売機から飲み物を取り出す。）

Lesson 14
Words and Phrases
1. uniform　　2. …なしで〜しない　　3. include
4. appearance　　5. 年の割に
6. 〜することに慣れている　　7. judge
8. society　　9. （規則など）を守る　　10. law

Questions
1. She was surprised at the school rules there.

解説 質問文は「大阪の高校を訪れたときにサラは

何に驚いたか」をたずねている。答えは本文第1
段落の I found a lot of surprising rules … 以下
を参考にする。

2. They should wear their school uniforms, shoes and neckties.

解説 質問文は「生徒たちは毎日学校で何を身につ
けるべきか」をたずねている。本文の1つ目の校
則を参照する。

3. He or she must do some cleaning after school.

解説 質問文は「5回遅刻したら何をするのか」を
たずねている。本文の5つ目の校則を参照する。

4. He thinks they are necessary because the children can learn the importance of obeying laws.

解説 記事にコメントをしているアラスターの日本
の校則に対する考えと理由をたずねている問題。
彼の考えは Rules are necessary … が示し，理由
は，コメント後半の「校則を守る理由を学ぶ機会
がないと，法律を守る重要性がわからない」に示
されている。

Express Yourself
例：You should wear sunglasses to protect your
eyes when you play outside at school.
The UV rays in sunshine are getting stronger
and stronger.　（24 words）

和訳 学校で外で遊ぶときには，目を守るためにサ
ングラスをかけるべきです。
日光の紫外線がますます強くなっています。

Lesson 15
Words and Phrases
1. （生涯の，または専門的な）職業　　2. weekend
3. grandparent　　4. 焼いた　　5. 建築士
6. experience　　7. helpful　　8. editor
9. lawyer　　10. スピーチをする（≒give a speech）

Questions
1. He liked the roast beef that his grandfather cooked very much.

別解：He liked the chocolate cake that Diana brought to the lunch.

解説 質問文は「サンデーランチでバリーが気に入
ったものは何か」である。第1段落に，バリーが
気に入ったものとして，ローストビーフとチョコ
レートケーキの2点が記述されているので，その
どちらかを書けばよい。

2. They are looking for some people who can talk about their jobs.

解説 質問文は「バリーの先生方はだれを探してい
るか」である。第2段落の最後の文に注目する。

3. She is an architect.

解説 質問文は「ダイアナの仕事は何か」である。ダイアナの職業を問われているので，解答する場合には，It (= Diana's job) is … も考えられるが，She is … がよいだろう。

4. He asks her to come to his school and talk about her job in front of the students.

解説 質問文は「バリーはダイアナに来月何をするようにお願いしているか」である。第3段落でバリーがダイアナに，Would you come to our school and … と頼んでいる。

Express Yourself

例：Hi, Mr. Ishiguro. How are you doing? We are going to hold a class reunion at our junior high school next month. If you can join us, please let me know. Thank you! (33 words)

和訳 イシグロ先生，こんにちは。お元気ですか。私たちは来月，中学校で同窓会を開催します。もし同窓会に出席できる場合は，お知らせください。よろしくお願いします。

Lesson 16

Words and Phrases

1. 先日　　2. stand　　3. 驚いたことに
4. quickly　　5. traditional
6. …のように見える　　7. ～するのをためらう
8. 花火　　9. impress　　10. expect

Questions

1. Mariko did.

解説 質問文は「だれがこの記事の筆者を，日本の夏祭りに連れて行ってくれたか」という主語を問う問題。「だれが」という主語をたずねているので〈主語＋(助)動詞〉の形で答える。

2. She ate *yakisoba*, which was Japanese fried noodles.

解説 質問文は「筆者が祭りで何を食べたか」をたずねている。本文第2段落より，焼きそばを食べたことがわかる。

3. Because they were moving around too quickly.

解説 質問文は「なぜ筆者が金魚をまったく捕まえることができなかったのか」という理由をたずねており，第2段落の最終文がその理由にあたる。

4. She bought a candied apple at the stand between the goldfish-scooping stand and the cotton-candy stand.

解説 質問文は「筆者は花火を見る前にどこで何を買ったか」をたずねている。第4段落の3文目に注目する。「金魚すくいの屋台とわたあめの屋台の間にある屋台でりんご飴を買った」と答える。

Express Yourself

例：You should see Japanese fireworks. They look beautiful in the night sky. Also, Japanese fireworks are known as some of the best fireworks in the world. (26 words)

和訳 あなたは日本の花火を見るべきです。それは夜空できれいに見えるからです。また，日本の花火は世界で最もよい花火として知られているからです。

Lesson 17

Words and Phrases

1. island　　2. …の北に　　3. scenery
4. まるで…であるかのように　　5. 浮かぶ
6. ～することをあきらめる　　7. rent
8. 景色のよい　　9. 道に迷う　　10. someday

Questions

1. It is located to the north of the mainland of Rakouzhia.

解説 質問文は「メロニー島はどこに位置しているか」である。第1段落第1文に注目する。

2. She enjoyed (seeing) the beautiful scenery.

解説 質問文は「筆者は島に行く列車の中で何を楽しんだか」をたずねている。第1段落最終文を参考にする。

3. They went to a local café and enjoyed coffee and sweets.

解説 質問文は「その夫婦は2日目の午後に何をしたか」である。第3段落の第2文に「地元のカフェに行き，コーヒーとスイーツを楽しんだ」とある。

4. They rented a car and drove around the island.

解説 質問文は「その夫婦は最後の日にどのように島をまわったか」である。第4段落の第1文に答えの根拠がある。

Express Yourself

例：My Travel Plan for Okinawa
I'm planning to go to Shurijo and look at the inside of the castle. After that, I'll go swimming in the sea. In the evening, I want to have Okinawa noodles. (31 words)

和訳 私は首里城に行って，その城の中を見ることを計画しています。その後，私は海に泳ぎに行くつもりです。夕方には，私は沖縄そばを食べたいです。

Lesson 18

Words and Phrases

1. …に関心がある　　2. 別々に　　3. activity
4. …を共通して持つ　　5. finally
6. personality　　7. ただちに
8. …が驚いたことに　　9. wife　　10. 特徴

Questions

1. They have an interest in them as a subject of their research.

解説 質問文は「科学者が双子にどんな関心をもっているか」である。第2段落1文目のWe scientists have long had ...の部分に注意する。

2. They were asked three (questions).

解説 質問文は「第2段落で，2組の双子はいくつの質問を問われたか」である。how they spent their time together, what subjects they liked, to talk about their own personality の3つを筆者からたずねられた。

3. It was that both twins said almost the same thing about their personalities.

解説 質問文は「何が筆者にとって最も興味深かったか」である。第2段落の最後の3文の内容を，質問に合わせた形にして答える。

4. They were surprised at the facts that their wives had the same name and that their children were born on the same day and had the same name.

解説 質問文は「40年間会っていなかった1組の双子が驚いたこと」を問うている。第3段落の3，4文の内容をまとめる。

Express Yourself

例：Subject ① Mathematics

I like mathematics because it is interesting for me to solve math problems by using equations.

Subject ② English

I like speaking English. I sometimes visit my ALT and talk to her in English. It's really fun!

Subject ③ Home Economics

I am good at home economics because I usually do the housework at home.

和訳 Subject ① 数学：私は数学が好きです。なぜなら方程式を使って数学の問題を解くのがおもしろいからです。Subject ② 英語：私は英語を話すのが好きです。私はときどきALTの先生のところを訪れ，彼女に英語で話しかけています。それはとても楽しいです。Subject ③ 家庭科：私は家庭科が得意です。なぜなら私はふだん家で家事をしているからです。

Lesson 19

Words and Phrases

1. …に精通している[…をよく知っている]
2. 典型的な　　3. probably　　4. 適切に
5. enter　　6. …をふく　　7. …が～できるように

8. rude　　9. …に満足している
10. ～するのを避ける

Questions

1. It is used for wiping our hands.

解説 質問文は what ... for?「なぜ…」と目的をたずねる表現で「日本のレストランではおしぼりは何のために使われるか」を問うている。第2段落2文目の You use it to wipe ... がポイント。It is used for ...に続く形になるので動名詞にする。

2. Because it is rude to do so [that].

解説 質問文は「なぜアメリカでは食事中に音を立ててはいけないのか」である。この理由は第3段落1文目に書いてある。模範解答のように to do so [that]（そうすること）をつけるとよい。

3. We should make a sipping sound to show that we are content with the ceremony.

解説 質問文は「茶会の終わりに抹茶を飲むとき，なぜすする音を立てるのか」である。模範解答のように本文の表現を使うこともできるが，別解として，... to show that we are satisfied with the ceremony. なども考えられる。

4. Because it is believed to bring bad luck.

解説 質問文は「なぜ2組の箸で食べ物をつかむことを避けるべきか」である。これは第4段落の第3文に答えの根拠がある。

Express Yourself

例：It is polite to say "itadakimasu" before you start to eat and to say "gochisosama deshita" when you finish eating. These phrases show our gratitude for the meal. （28 words）

和訳 食べ始める前に「いただきます」と言い，食べ終わるときに「ごちそうさまでした」と言うと，礼儀正しいです。これらのフレーズは食事に対する私たちの感謝を表しています。

Lesson 20

Words and Phrases

1. …に損害を与える　　2. 環境　　3. product
4. 何年も前に　　5. …を守る　　6. 計画
7. influence　　8. AだけでなくBも
9. 名所を見物する　　10. except

Questions

1. We recycle newspapers and plastic bottles.

解説 質問文は「私たちは環境に損害を与えないように何をリサイクルしているか」である。第1段落2文目に注目する。

2. Three (purposes) are.

解説 第2段落3文目に It has three main purposes. とある。この It は "ecotourism" を指す。

3. Because we will not only see the sights but also feel closer to them.

解説 質問文は「訪れようとしている場所の文化と歴史を学ぶことはなぜ大切なのか」である。本文の第4段落2文目に注目し，その理由を述べた3文目を参考にする。

4. They will smile and become friendly toward us.

解説 質問文は「地元の人々に地元の言語を使うと，何が起こるか」である。第4段落4，5文目に注目する。設問文の the local language は本文の the native language を指す。

Express Yourself

例：I would like to book a ship cruise from Queenstown. I am looking forward to seeing the beauty of the Fiordland National Park and Milford Sound!（26 words）

別解：I would like to reserve a dolphin tour in Kaikoura! I'll be really excited to see dolphins! I hope I can swim with them as well. That will be fantastic!（30 words）

和訳 私はクイーンズタウンからの船のクルージングを予約したいと思います。私はフィヨルドランド国立公園とミルフォードサウンドの美しい景色を眺めるのを楽しみにしています。

別解：私はカイコウラからのイルカツアーを予約したいです。イルカを見てとてもわくわくするでしょう。さらに，イルカといっしょに泳げることを願っています。それはすばらしいでしょう。

Lesson 21
Words and Phrases
1. graduate   2. perform   3. まれな
4. busy   5. 印象   6. これは…だからだ
7. …に影響を与える   8. create   9. 過去に
10. たとえ…しても

Questions
1. He started working as a musician.

解説 質問文は「筆者は大学卒業後，何をしたか」をたずねている。第1段落第1文に注目する。

2. He worked there for twenty years.

解説 質問文は「筆者はニューヨークでどのくらいの間働いたか」をたずねている。第1段落の第5文を参考にして答えを作るとよい。

3. It was that technology controlled the city.

解説 質問文は「筆者の東京の第一印象は何か」である。第2段落の第3，4文を参考にする。

4. He mainly uses computers when composing music.

解説 質問文は「筆者は現在，どのように作曲をす

るか」をたずねている。これは第4段落の第4文に答えの根拠がある。

Express Yourself

例：I would like to go to university in London to improve my English and communication skills because I want to work globally in the future.（25 words）

和訳 私は将来グローバルに働きたいと思っているので，ロンドンの大学に行って，英語とコミュニケーションの能力を高めたいです。

Lesson 22
Words and Phrases
1. 新聞記者   2. ますます…   3. …を設計する
4. 装置   5. cash   6. remain   7. 安全な
8. 尽きる   9. …に頼る   10. possibly

Questions
1. We can put them on our mobile devices, such as smartphones.

解説 質問文は「モバイルウォレットをどこに入れておくことができるか」である。第1段落の2文目に They are usually designed to run on mobile devices, such as smartphones. とある。

2. We should know several advantages and disadvantages of them.

解説 質問文は「モバイルウォレットを使い始める前にあなたは何をすべきか」である。第1段落3文目に注目する。

3. Because we don't have to take money out of our traditional wallets.

別解：Because we don't have to count the number of coins we use.

解説 質問文は「なぜモバイルウォレットを使うとよりすばやく支払いができるのか」である。Advantages の3. に注目して答えを作る。別解のように「硬貨を数えなくてよい」も答えとなる。

4. Because they may not really feel they are spending money.

解説 質問文は「モバイルウォレットを使うと，なぜもしかしたらお金を使い過ぎてしまうか」をたずねている。これは Disadvantages の2. に注目して答えを作る。

Express Yourself

例：More and more people in Japan are using electronic money. The number of electronic money payments in 2018 increased by about 3 billion from 2012.（25 words）

和訳 日本ではますますたくさんの人々が電子マネーを使っています。2018年の電子マネーの決済件数は，2012年より約30億件増加しました。